NO NONSENSE FINANCIAL GUIDE™

THE TRUTH ABOUT
MORTGAGES

M. J. Abadie

Cover design by Nancy Sabato

Interior design by Richard Oriolo

Library of Congress Cataloging-in-Publication Data

Abadie, M.J.
   No nonsense financial guide : the truth about mortgages / M.J. Abadie.—1st ed.
      p. cm.
   Includes bibliographical references and index.
   ISBN 0-681-41795-1
   1. Mortgage loans—United States.   2. Housing—United States—Finance.   I. Title.
   HG2040.5.U5A623   1993
   332.7'22'0973—dc20   92-42357
                                                           CIP

Printed in United States of America

First Edition

0 9 8 7 6 5 4 3 2 1

The Truth About Mortgages

THE NO NONSENSE LIBRARY

Dedicated to my nephews
Victor Hugo Abadie III
of Montara, California
and
James Paul Abadie
of Houston, Texas

Contents

INTRODUCTION

FINANCING YOUR HOME
WITH A MORTGAGE

Today's mortgage picture is much more complex than formerly. Banks and other financial institutions offer an often bewildering range of choices in the mortgage field. The days when the standard thirty-year, fixed-rate mortgage was the only option are gone forever. As the economy continues to go through worldwide changes, lenders will become increasingly creative in the products they offer, and the borrower's choices will increase accordingly.

Getting the mortgage you want should not cause you to endure sleepless nights or the endless torture of wondering if you are doing the right thing. By arming yourself with a basic knowledge of the mortgage financing options available, and by taking a careful and thorough look at your financial situation—both your needs and your housing goals—you will be able to apply with a clear head and an easy mind for the mortgage that fits your special requirements.

Selecting a mortgage is like buying a well-tailored suit. It must fit both the lender and the borrower without any part of the agreement giving discomfort. It must be roomy enough for comfort but tight enough for good wear.

To get a good mortgage fit, you must have a fairly comprehensive idea of what you wish to achieve and of what you can afford. The lending institution will want your precise financial measurements.

Many people think only of the rate of interest on their mortgage, but this is only one indicator of a proper fit. For some, a higher rate of interest may serve them better, or it may prove to be the only available option for their circumstances.

In order to choose intelligently among the many mortgage features on the market today, it's important to examine them carefully. *Shop around* should be the motto of the prospective buyer. Ask questions. Visit lending institutions in your area with the understanding that you have the right to make your own decision to your own best advantage. Often people—especially first-time users of mortgages—feel overwhelmed or intimidated by imposing financial institutions. However, they are there to serve you as well as to ensure their own profits. If you don't borrow, they don't profit. It's that simple.

Choosing the right mortgage can make your life simpler and easier in the long run. It may even enable you to buy the house of your dreams earlier than you thought possible. Putting the time and effort into selecting your mortgage to ensure a proper fit is one of the best investments you can make, as the work you do looking into home financing options will increase both your consumer power and your sense of security.

ONE

USING A MORTGAGE TO BUY A HOUSE

THE AMERICAN DREAM

Home ownership is an integral part of the American Dream. Nearly everyone longs to own a home—whether it's a suburban colonial, a tree-shaded Victorian brownstone, a low-rise co-op, a high-rise condominium, or a simple country cottage.

In the 1980s, the American Dream evolved into a new way of thinking. The vision of home ownership used to be not only that of owning one's own home but also of having it appreciate in value sufficiently to easily outpace inflation as the years went by. However, in today's changing economy and market Americans are beginning to realize their dream of home ownership differently.

Today, instead of approaching home ownership as a major growth investment with a huge potential for appreciation, Americans are increasingly looking on a home as their primary asset, one that provides the dual satisfaction of owning a home that reflects personal taste and fulfills family needs while still offering a moderate return.

This newly revised version of the American Dream is still underpinned by the traditional mortgage concept. As the purchase of a home is the single largest investment most people make in their lifetimes, choosing a mortgage is clearly an important financial decision.

Trends of the 1990s

According to *Money* magazine, which interviewed dozens of real estate brokers, builders, furnishings retailers, housing analysts, and demographers for the survey, summarized below, there are seven major housing trends for the 1990s.

1) *As incomes rise nationally, house prices will appreciate more than in the 1980s but less than in the 1970s.* Appreciation rates for homes will just about equal the inflation rate's expected 4.8 percent annual pace.

2) *Though the appreciation rate on houses will be less than in former decades, the home itself will become more important.* As the baby boomers age and become parents, the trend will be toward the home as a nesting place for family and friends.

3) *More people will be able to afford to purchase a home.* The baby boomers are reaching their

prime earning years and are more likely to be able to afford a home now.

4) *In many regions there will be a buyers' market over a sellers' market,* partly because the new agency created by the savings and loan bailout, the Resolution Trust Corporation, will be disposing of its huge inventory of repossessed single-family homes formerly owned by the bankrupt thrifts.

5) *Lenders will be eager to accommodate buyers and will provide more and better—including speedier—services, and there may be single-digit mortgage rates for much of the decade.* Experts expect to see mortgage interest rates driven down by a flood of capital, perhaps to as low as 7 percent by the mid-1990s. Financial institutions will lure customers by making fast approvals available.

6) *Brokerage commissions will go down.* The number of real estate agents has risen, while the number of listings has fallen, lowering commissions below the once-standard 6 percent.

7) *Environmental concerns will affect mortgages.* In future, newly built homes will have to conform to environmental standards in order to get financing for them.

WHO SHOULD MORTGAGE?

Experts agree that there is no such thing as a typical mortgage client. People who use mortgages to buy a house—whether it is a first home or they are "trading up" to a bigger and better one—come from all walks of life and live in widely varying circumstances. Thus, lending institutions offer a wide range of fixed- and adjustable-rate mortgages to provide for the purchase or refinancing of primary residences, one- or multiple-family homes, vacation homes, condominiums, and cooperative apartments.

Before deciding to use a mortgage, it's important to do an analysis of your personal and financial goals. Here are some questions to ask yourself.

1) Are you looking to build equity quickly?
2) Are you expecting your income to increase and, if so, by how much and when?
3) How long can you confidently plan to stay in the home you want to purchase?
4) Might a career change or other circumstances arise that would necessitate a move? If so, when?
5) Should a move become necessary, would you sell the home or keep it—perhaps as a rental property?
6) How will the tax deductions from your home's interest payments affect your general tax situation, now and in the future?
7) Will you be making major improvements on the house? If so, when, how much will they cost, and how will you finance them?
8) Do you have a steady income?
9) What is your employment record?
10) Have you any secondary income?
11) How much debt do you carry, and of what sort—credit cards, auto payments, alimony, child support, etc.?

12) What is your current net worth?
13) What is your credit history?
14) How much income do you have available for mortgage payments each month without strain?
15) What amount of down payment are you planning to make?
16) Are you borrowing for the down payment or do you have the money in hand?
17) Have you gone bankrupt or been foreclosed in the past seven years?
18) Are you adequately covered by insurance?
19) Do you have a retirement plan?
20) Do you have the equivalent of three to six months' income in a savings account or money market fund?

The answers to these questions will help you to see whether you are someone who should seek a mortgage.

THE AFFORDABLE HOUSE

It's a good idea to have an accurate idea of how much you can put down and how much you can afford in monthly payments before you start looking for a house to buy. Although there are many options available to borrowers that may enable them to buy a more expensive house than they think they can afford, it helps greatly to know what your upper boundaries are.

Ordinarily, with a down payment of 10 to 20 percent of the purchase price, a buyer can consider a property that is no more than 2 1/2 times his gross annual family income. This rule of thumb is only a ballpark figure. In actual practice, a lender wants to know about your ability to repay the loan.

When going house shopping, keep in mind that there are three major factors a lender will consider when you apply for your mortgage. These are:

1) the current market value of the property
2) your ability to repay the loan
3) your credit history

The Down Payment

Because the lender's security for repayment of the loan is the property itself, no lender wants to lend 100 percent of the property's current market value. This is why a down payment is required from the buyer. The higher the down payment, the lower the lender's risk and the more likely he is to approve the loan. Generally speaking, the common practice is for lenders to lend 80 percent of the property's value. Thus, 20 percent of the appraised value is usually required for a down payment.

However, there are lenders who will write mortgages with higher loan-to-value ratios (that is, with smaller down payments), particularly if the borrower procures private mortgage insurance as a protection against possible default. The PMI premium is usually added to the monthly payment—which, of course, means a larger payment.

In addition, some lenders are willing to write mortgage loans with as little as 10 percent down payment without mortgage insurance, but usually they charge somewhat higher interest rates and fees to protect their investment.

The primary advantage of this high loan-to-value rate is that the additional interest may be tax deductible, whereas the fees paid for mortgage insurance may not be deductible.

How Much Home Can You Afford?

Find the intersection of ANNUAL GROSS INCOME and QUALIFYING INTEREST RATE for an estimate of the sales price of a home for which you may qualify.* The sales prices are both adjustable (upper figure) and fixed rate (lower figure) mortgage.

80% LTV					90% LTV				
Annual Gross Income	Qualifying Interest Rate				Annual Gross Income	Qualifying Interest Rate			
	7%	8%	9%	10%		7%	8%	9%	10%
$20,000	90	85	75	70	$20,000	75	70	65	60
	70	65	60	55		65	55	50	45
$30,000	135	125	115	110	$30,000	115	110	100	95
	105	100	90	85		90	85	75	70
$40,000	185	170	155	145	$40,000	155	145	135	125
	145	130	120	110		120	110	105	95
50,000	230	210	195	180	$50,000	195	180	170	155
	180	165	150	140		155	140	130	120
$60,000	275	255	235	220	$60,000	235	220	205	190
	215	200	185	170		185	170	155	145
$80,000	370	340	315	295	$80,000	315	295	270	250
	290	265	245	225		245	225	210	195
$100,000	465	425	395	365	$100,000	395	365	340	315
	360	305	300	285		310	285	265	245

Sales prices in $000

Figures based on 30 Year Amortization and 80% or 90% Loan to Value (LTV). Figures based on Principal, Interest, Taxes and Insurance (PITI). 90% Loans include one-half percent (50 basis points) for mortgage insurance. Association fees or other housing costs not included. Annual taxes based on 1% of Sales Price. Monthly insurance based on .035% of Loan Amount. Figures rounded down to nearest $5,000. Front End Qualifying Ratios used for both 80% and 90% Loans: 36% Adjustable, 28% Fixed Monthly PITI/Gross Monthly Income= Housing Qualifying Ratio.

*Qualifying for a loan requires much more than simply meeting front-end ratios. This chart is merely an aid to estimate the sales price of a home at varying levels of buyer income and interest rates, and to show the difference between an Adjustable Rate Mortgage and a Fixed Rate Mortgage. These calculations are estimates only.

SOURCE: Home Savings of America

The result of all this is the following formula: the more money you put down, the less you'll need to borrow, the less your monthly payments will be, and the more equity you have starting from the day you assume ownership.

Your Monthly Payment

Charts I and II will give you an indication of what an affordable monthly payment is and if your monthly income can cover it along with the rest of your major expenses.

This chart lets you estimate your monthly payment. Simply divide your gross monthly income (before taxes) by three. (Dividing gross income by three is a convenient rule of thumb used by lenders to ascertain whether your monthly payment exceeds what they consider to be the proper proportion.) Your total housing expenses should not be more than one-third of your gross income. Although not rigid, this formula is the one used by many financial analysts and lending institutions.

CHART I:
Estimated Monthly Housing Expense

1. Monthly *gross* income $ _____
2. Divide by three $ _____

The second figure represents your *estimated* afford-able monthly housing expense, and it includes your monthly real estate tax and home insurance payments in addition to your monthly loan payment (both principal and interest).

CHART II:
Figuring Monthly Expenses

1. Monthly *net* income $ _____
   (include after-tax wages, interest income, dividends, alimony, etc.)
2. Estimated monthly housing expense $ _____
   (Make a list of all your monthly expenses—food, clothing, utilities, transportation, installment payments, insurance, medical and dental costs, household items, etc.)
3. Subtract the amount in Line 2 from the amount in Line 1 $ _____

The amount on Line 3 of Chart II is how much you'll have left over to meet your other monthly expenses after paying your estimated mortgage payment. If the amount on Line 3 is equal to or (ideally) less than the amount on Line 2,

you will know you can comfortably afford the estimated
housing costs each month.

FINDING THE AFFORDABLE HOUSE

This table shows the approximate monthly payments for a
thirty-year, fixed-rate mortgage for different priced
houses, with 10 percent and 20 percent down payments at
various interest rates. To find the total cost of home
ownership, you will need to add real estate taxes, any
applicable co-op or condo maintenance fees, and hazard
or mortgage insurance.

Cost of House	Down Payment	Approximate Monthly Principal and Interest Payment Would Be				
		7%	8%	9%	10%	11%
$ 80,000	$ 8,000	$ 480	$528	$579	$632	$686
	16,000	425	470	515	562	609
150,000	15,000	898	991	1,086	1,185	1,286
	30,000	798	881	966	1,053	1,143
200,000	20,000	1,197	1,321	1,448	1,580	1,714
	40,000	1,065	1,174	1,287	1,404	1,524

The table below will give you an idea of what your
equity-debt ratio would be at five-year intervals on a
mortgage of $150,000. For purposes of illustration, the
table is based on a thirty-year, fixed-rate mortgage.

Equity-Debt Ratio

Year	Equity	Debt Remaining	Total Value
1	$ 50,683	$ 99,317	$150,000
5	54,120	95,880	150,000
10	60,570	98,430	150,000
15	70,670	79,330	150,000
20	86,482	63,518	150,000
25	111,239	38,761	150,000
30	150,000	0	150,000

Debt represents the balance remaining due on the entire mortgage. *Equity* equals the purchase price on the house less the debt, i.e., the amount which you own at any given time.

Mortgage Money for Property Other than a House

Mortgages can be used for the purchase of other property, such as boats and trailers, and the same general rules apply. However, generally speaking, much less money is involved, and therefore considerations differ. What is significant is that the property is used to secure the loan and failure to make payments can result in loss of the property.

TWO

KINDS OF MORTGAGES

After examining your housing needs and calculating your ability to afford them, you are now ready to consider the mortgage that satisfies the full range of your goals.

Real estate financing is one of many investment possibilities. Although in some cases borrowers with limited finances have little or no choice in the type of loan they can qualify for and afford, many people do have a range of options from which to choose. It makes sense to seek and select a mortgage that gives you the best possible arrangement in terms of interest, monthly payments, debt reduction, inflation, and taxes. You can even restructure your mortgage later on if you wish.

Some mortgages have "fixed rate"; that is, the rate and payment amount remain constant for the duration of the loan. Others have "adjustable rates" and offer more flexibility; their rates and payment schedules can adjust to reflect changing economic factors. Still others offer a convertiblity factor, enabling the borrower to convert from one type of loan to another after a period of time.

It's important to understand the different types of mortgages in today's market in order to evaluate which most adequately meets your particular needs.

FIXED-RATE MORTGAGES

With a fixed-rate mortgage, your interest rate and monthly payment remain the same over the life of the mortgage.

Each month your payment includes interest plus a predetermined amount of your loan balance so that, at maturity, your entire loan will have been repaid and you will own your property outright. This type of loan calculation is called a "fixed amortization schedule."

Ordinarily, lenders offer a choice between a fifteen-year loan and a thirty-year loan. With the shorter time period, the monthly payments are larger but the total interest costs are less because the money is borrowed for a shorter time period. Also, with a shorter time period, you build equity faster and, of course, pay off the loan faster.

However, the lower payment schedule for a thirty-year loan can make a mortgage easier to qualify for if your monthly income is not sufficient to ensure making the larger payment. The downside of the lower payment schedule for the thirty-year loan is that the interest rates are generally higher, as the lender is risking his investment over a longer term.

The key feature of the fixed-rate mortgage is its *predictability*. As the borrower, you have the knowledge that your rate and payment will never change as long as you have the loan—a feature that makes it much easier to plan finances and budget over the years.

Unfortunately, that comfortable feature of predictability may carry a higher price tag. As it's extremely difficult for lenders to predict where interest rates will go over fifteen or thirty years, they often attempt to offset this factor by quoting higher interest rates, higher monthly payments, and higher loan fees than for other types of mortgage financing.

The table below will let you figure out the monthly payment necessary to pay off a fixed-rate loan at different rates of interest. The figures in the table represent principal and interest only and do not include property taxes or insurance.

How to Use the Table

1. Choose the interest rate quoted by your lender in column at far right.
2. Find the term of years you want, reading across.
3. Multiply the figure in the term-of-years column by the number of thousands of dollars you plan to borrow; for example, if you have been quoted an interest rate of 11 percent for thirty years on $100,000, you would multiply 9.53 by 100, giving a total of $953.00. This amount would be your approximate monthly payment.

Estimated Mortgage Payments for Fixed-Rate Loans

Interest Rate	15 Years	20 Years	25 Years	30 Years	40 Years
7%	8.99	7.76	7.07	6.66	6.22
8%	9.56	8.37	7.72	7.34	6.96
9%	10.15	9.00	8.40	8.05	7.72
10%	10.75	9.66	9.09	8.78	8.50
11%	11.37	10.33	9.81	9.53	9.29
12%	12.01	11.02	10.54	10.29	10.09
13%	12.66	11.72	11.28	11.27	10.90

Source: Home Savings of America

The following table shows how a fixed-rate loan, over a period of thirty years, might be paid.

Fixed-Rate Amortization Table

Mortgage Value $100,000.00
Interest Rate 9.00%
Term (years) 30%
Monthly Payment $804.62

Year	Month	Amount of Interest	Principal Reduction	Remaining Balance
1	12	$745.32	($59.30)	$99,316.80
5	60	$719.74	($84.88)	$95,880.14
10	120	$671.72	($132.90)	89,429.74
15	180	$596.54	($208.08)	$79,330.49
20	240	$478.83	($325.79)	$63,518.27
25	300	$294.54	($510.09)	$38,761.39
30	360	$5.99	($798.63)	$0.00

ADJUSTABLE-RATE MORTGAGES

Adjustable-rate mortgages, as the name implies, have interest rates that fluctuate. They are tied to, and reflect changes in, a published financial index. As those index rates fluctuate—up or down—ARM rates follow. The lender is prohibited by law from controlling the rate index he uses. For example, a bank is not allowed to hitch its ARM rates to its prime rate.

Below are some terms used in describing ARMs with which you should be familiar before discussing your mortgage requirements with a potential lender.

The index There are a number of indexes, and some of them move sharply over relatively short time spans. Others change more slowly over longer periods of time. The two most widely used indexes are:

- TREASURY RATE INDEXES. These track the current interest rates the U.S. government pays to borrow money (the yield on Treasury bills, notes, and bonds). Determined at the weekly auctions the government uses to sell its securities, interest rates pegged to the Treasury rate have been known to fluctuate dramatically in response to changes—or expected changes—in the economy. As a result, ARM mortgages tied to this index can fluctuate just as widely.

- COST OF FUNDS INDEXES. These are based on average interest rates savings institutions nationwide pay to their depositors. Historically these indexes have operated within a narrower range than the Treasury indexes, and they move much more slowly. The reason is that they reflect the institutions' *costs* rather than their new or maturing deposit rates. As savings accounts do mature at differing times, rates cannot change drastically, which explains the slow movement of a cost of funds index and mortgage rates that are adjusted by it.

One of these cost of funds indexes, used nationwide, is published by the Federal Home Loan Bank of San Francisco. It is called the 11th District Cost of Funds Index (COFI), and it reflects the borrowing costs of approximately two hundred savings and loan associations in California, Nevada, and Arizona.

The Margin An ARMS interest rate is a reflection of both the index to which it is pegged and a margin added by the lender to cover costs of operation and ensure profit, usually from 2.25 to 3 percent. The margin is fixed at the time of the loan and cannot be changed during its duration.

Start Rate This is the rate of interest applicable at the beginning of the loan's term. It can be in effect for as long as several years or as short as a month.

Interest Rate Adjustment Frequency Once the start rate lapses, interest rates are adjusted according to the index. Depending on the structure of the loan, the lender, and the index, an ARM rate may be adjusted monthly, semiannually, or annually. Usually, the shorter the time period used for the adjustment frequency, the smaller the payment change is likely to be. However, although the lender may have the right to adjust the rate monthly, this is rare. In practice, it is more likely that the adjustment will occur at longer intervals. In either case, rate adjustment does not necessarily mean that the monthly *payment* will rise or fall; payment changes may be restricted to once a year or once in six months, depending on the annual payment cap.

Annual Payment Cap This option provides the borrower with protection by putting an annual cap on the amount his payment can change. The maximum increase is usually 7.5 percent of the previous year's monthly payment. As a general rule of thumb, 7.5 percent approximates a 1 percent change in the interest rate. Payments are not allowed to exceed the cap, regardless of what the index shows during the year. For example, if your monthly payment is $1,000, it cannot be increased to more than $1,075 in the following year.

Interest Rate Adjustment Caps Some ARMs do not have an annual payment cap feature. Ordinarily, these will offer an annual cap of up to 2 percent on interest rate adjustments, especially if the ARM is pegged to a Treasury index. Note that a 2 percent interest increase can translate into a payment increase of as much as 15 to 20 percent.

Lifetime Interest Rate Cap This feature, offered with most ARMs, puts an absolute ceiling on the rate by which an ARM loan can be adjusted over the life of the loan. Should the rate reach the maximum, the ARM converts to a fixed-rate loan at that rate until the index falls below it, at which time the rate is then adjusted downward. ARMs that offer a maximum cap usually demand a minimum interest rate as well.

Negative Amortization Option It is possible with an ARM loan that the monthly payment, after adjustment, will not be sufficient to pay the full amount of interest due. If, for example, the adjusted monthly payment is $700 but

$735 is required to cover the interest, the borrower has the choice of either paying the extra amount of $35.00 each month or having it accrue to his loan balance. This is an important option. Without it, the borrower has no choice but to pay the additional amount monthly, thus raising the payment account.

Principal Cap With the negative amortization option, it is possible for the loan balance to grow considerably over a period of years. With this in mind, a principal cap is usually established—125 percent of the original loan amount is a normal cap. If, for example, the original loan was $100,000 and because of the use of negative amortization the loan balance has increased to above $125,000, the borrower will have to make a lump-sum payment to keep below the cap.

Accelerated Amortization This is the opposite of negative amortization. This feature, which is one of the benefits of an ARM, provides one-year fixed-payment periods. Thus, when interest rates are falling, the loan balance gets paid down faster because more of the monthly payment goes to pay off the principal.

Loan Term As it is possible, with negative amortization, that the loan balance of an ARM may increase, many ARMs provide a built-in extension factor. Lenders will generally approve a loan extension of thirty to forty years, which eliminates the need to refinance or sell if one cannot come up with the lump-sum payment.

Loan Assumability ARMs can often be assumed by another borrower, unlike most fixed-rate mortgages. The interest rate is usually the same that was in effect on the loan at the time of assumption. This feature can be a valuable asset when you are ready to sell.

Prepayment Penalty No prepayment penalty is applicable on most ARM loans. They can be paid down partially or in full, giving the borrower the option of paying off the loan faster, if he chooses, in order to reduce interest costs.

<u>Long-term Options</u> As one of the negative features of an ARM is the possibility that the monthly payment may increase beyond affordability, lenders now offer a number of long-term ARMs:

- THE "TWO-STEP" MORTGAGE is a financial instrument backed by the Federal National Mortgage Association (Fannie Mae) under which the interest rate cannot increase more than 6 points over the term of the mortgage.

  Points are perhaps the most confusing cost at closing. Another name for a point is *loan discount fee*. A point is equal to 1 percent of a mortgage and is paid or credited to the lender at settlement. There is a seven-year first step, with an interest rate somewhat below fixed levels, followed by a twenty-three-year second step with interest set for the remaining life of the mortgage at the then-current rates.

  Although the two-step plan provides only one rate adjustment, that adjustment *can* be, in the worst-case scenario, a "payment shock." However, the two-step is a form of financing that is worth investigating.

  The two-step offers a stability similiar to that of fixed-rate financing, and it is a definite thirty-year commitment, whereas with other ARMs, some lenders demand a "bailout" clause that enables them to terminate the loan if interest rates rise above a certain level.

- OTHER LONG-TERM OPTIONS on ARM loans are:

    The 7/1 loan. Initial rate lasts seven years and then is adjusted annually.

    The 5/1 loan. Initial rate lasts five years and then is adjusted annually.

    The 3/1 loan. Initial rate lasts three years and then is adjusted annually.

    The 5/5 loan. Initial rate for five years and then adjusts to a new rate every five years thereafter.

    The 10/10/10 loan. Rates and payments can change every five to ten years.

In addition, some ARM loans are offered with terms of up to forty years. This longer term can make qualifying easier, and the longer term can mean smaller payments than a thirty-year loan.

Listed below are some examples of current prevalent types of ARMs.

Cost of Funds Index ARM with Negative Amortization Option

This ARM usually has a 7.5 percent annual payment cap to protect the borrower from "payment shock." Another popular feature of this type of ARM is a lower initial interest rate, which is usually fixed for the first six months. Afterward, it adjusts monthly in accordance with the cost of funds index.

Payments, however, remain the same for the first year and, because of the cap, cannot increase more then 7.5 percent over the next twelve months.

Many ARMs buyers cannot anticipate mortgage costs over the life of their loans, and this type of ARM offers the advantage of more control over payments.

The disadvantage is the use of negative amortization, which, although it allows control over payments, can have the effect of requiring the borrower to come up with a huge lump sum once the cap is reached. The problem with negative amortization is that you cannot depend on the loan being paid off during the thirty-year term, a factor that makes overall financial planning more difficult than with a fixed-rate mortgage.

Cost of Funds Index ARM Without Negative Amortization Option

Typically, this ARM has *no* annual payment cap. In place of the cap, it usually has an interest rate cap of 1 percent every six months, or up to 2 percent annually. In accordance with cost of funds index changes, rates are adjusted every six or twelve months, and payments adjust accordingly. Since you *always* pay at the current rate, even when it hikes up the payment considerably, you never have to worry about coming up with a large lump sum through using negative amortization.

T-Bill ARM Without Negative Amortization Option

This ARM is pegged to a Treasury index. In place of the usual annual payment cap, it carries a 2 percent annual interest rate cap. Adjustments of payments coincide with the Treasury interest rate every six or twelve months, thus eliminating the possibility of negative amortization.

ARMS used to be a free-for-all in the financial market, with thousands of products being available. This situation caused much confusion and made it difficult to sell such loans to secondary lenders, such as Fannie Mae. With experience behind them, ARMs providers are now offering more standardized products, available nationwide. This makes the ARM loan easier to evaluate.

ARMs, however, will remain a supplement to the fixed-rate, conventional mortgage. Fixed-rate returns are important to many segments of the general investment public—such as the managers of pension funds who need predictability in choosing investments. As investors purchase billions of dollars' worth of mortgages through secondary lenders, there is a continuing demand for fixed-rate loan products. This demand means that fixed-rate financing will remain viable and popular in the years to come.

The FHA ARM

One of the lesser-known ARMs is one developed by the FHA. This carries an annual payment cap of 1 percent, a feature that has not made it very attractive to lenders. Nevertheless, it is available in some areas and has some good features:

1) Interest costs can rise or fall 1 percent annually.
2) The interest rate cannot rise or fall more than 5percent over the initial rate.
3) The index to which the FHA ARM is pegged is selected by the government, usually based on one-year Treasury securities.
4) There is no negative amortization.
5) There is no prepayment penalty.
6) FHA ARMs are assumable using the same guidelines that pertain to any other FHA financing.

Some Things to Watch Out For

All ARMs are *not* created alike. There can be a seemingly bewildering variety of formats. Look out for:

- *"Balloon" payment at maturity*. The balloon is a large sum payable at the end of the loan term. The danger is that if the borrower fails to make the large final payment he could lose the property through foreclosure.
- ARMs that *do not have an annual payment cap or an annual interest rate cap*. This could spell uncontrollable fluctuations in payment and interest rates.
- ARMs with *no lifetime interest rate cap* should be rejected.
- Is the loan *assumable* by a qualified borrower? This is a vital question, especially if you might already know you will hold the property a shorter time than the term of the mortgage.
- ARMs that offer *discounts in return for an unusually high margin* are suspect and should be avoided.
- In general, borrowers should be extremely thorough in comparing programs offered by local lenders.

CONVERTIBLE MORTGAGE LOANS

Some lenders offer ARMs that allow for conversion to a fixed-rate loan at a specified time in the future—usually within the first five years.

The convertibility feature may bring with it a higher interest rate and/or higher processing fees.

Another factor is that, on conversion, the rate for your fixed loan may be higher than rates being offered on *new* fixed-rate mortgages. In addition, there may be a conversion fee.

However, there is another type of convertible loan that works in the opposite manner:

You can convert a fixed-rate loan to an ARM after five years. This type of loan may be one involving a larger than average amount of money. When interest rates are falling, this type of mortgage offers the advantage of locking in a favorable rate for five years and later, when the loan converts, enjoying rates and payment caps and assumability.

GRADUATED PAYMENT ADJUSTABLE RATE MORTGAGES (GPARM)

The GPARM is basically a mortgage with two phases. Usually for the first five years, monthly payments are set at a relatively low figure. The initial rate is below the market rate ordinarily offered on ARMs.

During the first phase, the payment level is advanced by a preset amount, such as 7.5 percent, while interest costs are pegged to an index. During this phase, negative authorization is allowed.

During the second phase, the GPARM is identical to a regular ARM in that the monthly payments remain fixed for certain intervals of one to five years and the interest fluctuates according to the index used. Payments may be adjusted up or down.

Remember, new loan programs are being introduced constantly. It's a good idea to ask both your real estate professional and your lender for current updates.

The following table shows how an adjustable-rate loan may vary over a five-year period.

Adjustable Rate Sample Payment Table
For First Five Years

$100,000 ARM
Thirty-year Term

Year	Interest Rate	Amount of Payment	Amount of Interest	Principal Reduction	Remaining Balance
1	7.0%	$7,983.60	$6,967.82	($1,015.78)	$98,984.22
2	8.0%	$8,789.16	$7,886.10	($903.06)	$98,081.16
3	9.0%	$9,655.44	$8,792.28	($863.16)	$97,218.00
4	9.5%	$10,013.76	$9,200.92	($812.84)	$96,405.16
5	9.0%	$9,651.68	$8,635.38	($1,016.30)	$95,388.86

Want More Information?

Get the "ARM Check Kit"

by writing to

HSH Associates

1200 Route 23

Butler, NJ 07405

The kit provides information that explains mortgage note clauses and details.

Or, consider also the use of an ARM examination service. Firms that provide ARM audits include:

Loantech   1-800-888-6781

Loancheck   1-619-464-8874

HSH Assoc.   1-800-873-2837

National Average Rates for the Most Common Mortgages, April 24, 1992

30-year fixed	8.93%	
15-year fixed	8.55%	
1-year ARM (Initial rate)		6.03%

SOURCE: HSH Associates

CHOOSING BETWEEN FIXED AND ADJUSTABLE RATES

Making the best choice among the financing options being offered means taking a careful look at your housing and financial goals.

Is the amount of the monthly payment the most important consideration in your financial planning?

Are security and stability chief among your needs, or do you have the flexibility to allow your interest rates to follow the market?

There is no single right answer for everybody, of course. Each individual family will have its own needs and its own requirements.

Primarily, the choice you make between a fixed-rate and an adjustable-rate mortgage will affect your monthly payments over the life of the loan. Make this decision after carefully considering your estimates of income and expenditures for the term of ownership you contemplate, whether it be short, long, or lifetime.

To be certain that the monthly payment for principal and interest will not vary during the term of your mortgage, choose a fixed-rate loan. This is especially advisable if you anticipate small increase in future income.

The longer you plan to hold on to your property, the more likely you are to benefit from a fixed-rate mortgage.

Conversely, if you expect to sell within five years or less, or if you expect interest rates to go down, the ARM, with its rate-changing features, might be more appealing. The principal advantage of an ARM for short-term home buyers is that the initial interest is usually lower than the best rate available on a fixed-rate mortgage.

The table below shows the percentages of fixed-rate and ARMs purchases by the Federal Home Loan Board nationwide.

Fixed- Versus Adjustable-Rate Mortgages $ Amounts Nationwide 1990

Type of Loan	Million $ Amounts	Percent
Fixed-Rate	57,207.40	77.8%
Adjustable-Rate	16,285.70	22.2%
Total	73,493.10	100.00%

For More Information

Call Investor Inquiry
Federal Home Loan Board
1-800-336-3672

Following is an indication of which loan types might be suitable for you . . . IF . . .

Fixed Rate If you believe interest rates will increase dramatically while you're in the home.

If you are living on a fixed income.

ARM: Cost of Funds Index with Negative Amortization Option If you believe that interest rates may decline or you are uncertain as to which direction they might go in the coming years.

If you want to have control over your monthly payments and avoid the possibility of payment shock.

If you want the option to either include all the interest you owe in your monthly payments or add it to your loan balance.

ARM: Cost of Funds Index Without Negative Amortization Option If you believe that interest rates may decline, or you are uncertain as to which direction they might go in the coming years.

If you want to be sure your payments cover the full amount of interest due in order to avoid negative amortization.

ARM: T-Bill Index Without Negative Amortization Option If you believe T-bill rates will remain stable or will decline in the near future.

Convertible: Adjustable- to Fixed-Rate If you want the flexibility to be able to convert to a fixed rate because you believe rates will be lower in the future.

Convertible: Fixed- to Adjustable-Rate If you want to lock into present rates and enjoy the benefits of an ARM.

A Comparison of Typical Loan Types

Type of Loan	Index[1]	Interest Rate Adjustment Frequency	Annual Payment Cap	Interest Rate Adjustment Cap	Lifetime Interest Rate Cap	Negative Amortization Option	Accelerated Amortization	Assumability	Prepayment Penalty
Fixed-Rate	None	None	N/A	N/A	N/A	No	No	No	Varies
ARM: Cost-of-Funds Index with Negative Amortization Option	Historically stable	Monthly, semi-annually, or annually	7½% of previous year's payment	None	Yes	Yes	Yes	Yes	No
ARM: Cost-of-Funds Index without Negative Amortization Option	Historically stable	Semi-annually or annually	None	2% annually	Yes	No	No	Yes	No
ARM: T-Bill Index without Negative Amortization Option	Historically stable	Semi-annually or annually	None	2% annually	Yes	No	No	Yes	No
Convertible: Adjustable- to Fixed-Rate	Historically stable	Semi-annually or annually during adjustable period	None	2% annually during adjustable period	Yes	No	No	Varies	No
Convertible: Fixed- to Adjustable-Rate[2]	Historically stable	Monthly, semi-annually, or annually during adjustable period	7½% of previous year's payment	None	Yes	Yes	Yes	Yes	No

[1] The fact that interest rates on ARMS more closely track the lender's costs will usually result in lower interest payments, loan fees and easier qualification requirements.

[2] The adjustable period is based on a Cost-of-Funds Index with negative amortization option.

Source: Home Savings of America

FHA LOANS

The Federal Housing Administration (FHA), one of the oldest and largest sources of mortgage assistance, offers programs to the general public. The FHA does not, however, lend money to home buyers. What it does instead is to guarantee repayment to participating lenders. This guarantee is so well-respected that borrowers on FHA programs can get excellent loan terms with very little money down. What is usually understood as "FHA financing" refers to the loans developed under Section 203-B, which is the largest of the many mortgage insurance programs sponsored by the FHA.

Generally speaking, to qualify for an FHA-backed loan, buyers must be financially qualified on the basis of *gross* income, and the property in question must be approved by an FHA appraiser.

As there are many complications and different rules and regulations for different FHA programs, check with your lender for the latest loan limits and other qualifications and restrictions that apply in your area.

VA FINANCING

Like the FHA, the VA (Veterans Administration) does not actually make loans but guarantees their repayment or a portion thereof. In effect, the VA acts as *cosigner* on loans to qualified individuals. Usually there is no down payment required on a VA loan, but the lender can require a down payment in order to process the mortgage, and although the VA does not limit mortgage amounts, lenders can and do limit what they will loan.

For complete information, active-duty personnel should contact their legal affairs officer. Nonduty personnel should contact their local VA offices. Information may vary according to the area in which you live.

THREE

OBTAINING A MORTGAGE

FINDING A LENDER

The first step in obtaining a mortgage is to find a qualified lender. *Locating* lenders should pose no problem. Nearly every type of financial institution offers some form of real estate financing because real estate is a quality investment.

However, be prepared to put in some time and effort to find the *right* lender for you. You may already have chosen the house you plan to buy, and you may know what type of financing you desire. The lender you want must be able to provide you with a mortgage at a competitive rate and should be able to process your application swiftly and accurately at a reasonable cost. In addition, you want to be assured that the lending institution is stable, experienced, and committed.

LENDER INSTITUTIONS

When going shopping for the best deal, it helps to know who makes loans, who facilitates the process, and what the various functions of the players are.

SAVINGS AND LOAN ASSOCIATIONS are specialized financial organizations that traditionally have been the primary, and largest, source of mortgages for personal residences.

Because savings and loans have been able to attract savings from the general public due to the fact that governmental regulations once gave them the right to pay higher interests than those of commercial banks, they have always been active in the mortgage market. Also, federal rules were such that savings and loans derived the best tax benefits by investing most of their available funds in mortgages.

In spite of the well-publicized fact that a number of savings and loans have gone under, those that remain—who generally have followed conservative policies by continuing to specialize in home loans—are a good mortgage source in most communities and a major source of financing for homes.

COMMERCIAL BANKS seem to be getting more and more involved in the mortgage loan business, although mortgages are still a secondary activity for them. However, because the residential mortgage business is a solid lending opportunity, banks are finding it increasingly attractive.

SAVINGS BANKS are today virtually indistinguishable from savings and loans. Formerly, savings banks could issue checks while savings and loans could not, but that difference was eliminated when NOW accounts were developed, giving savings and loans checking capability.

LIFE INSURANCE COMPANIES are a substantial mortgage source. However, most of their monies are used to finance large projects, such as shopping malls and apartment complexes, rather than single-unit family homes. Still, it is possible to have a home financed with insurance funds even though the loan ostensibly comes from elsewhere.

Since 1978, CREDIT UNIONS have been allowed to finance first mortgages. When certain restrictions were removed in 1982, credit unions began emerging as solid mortgage choices.

MORTGAGE BANKERS are individuals and institutions who use their own capital, as well as money from diverse sources, to create mortgages. They locate borrowers who meet the standards demanded by their investors, and they generally service the loans they make.

MORTGAGE BROKERS are individuals and institutions who match those needing loans with investors with available capital. Commercial real estate brokers often perform this function.

REAL ESTATE BROKERS are not actually lenders, but they are a real superior source of mortgage information. Both buyers and sellers are accustomed to using brokers to locate real estate financing and to give advice on loan formats currently available in their area.

SELLERS are sometimes the holders of financing. Such deals are particularly likely to be available when interest rates rise. Seller financing is always an individual matter.

ATTORNEYS are sometimes part of the loan process, even though they do not make loans themselves. They are used to review real estate agreements prior to final acceptance, and they often conduct the "closing" procedure. If an attorney has been involved in your transaction, he or she will accompany you to the closing.

THINGS YOU NEED TO KNOW
ABOUT A LENDER

As a guideline, below are some important questions to which you'll need answers when you select the right lender. Remember that different lending institutions have different policies. The policies of one may disqualify you, while those of another may allow you to borrow more than you need. Unfortunately, many borrowers, especially first-timers, feel intimidated about asking the questions they need to have answered, but the simple reality is that real estate financing is business. It's not a mysterious process, nor are you asking for a favor. If you cannot ask the tough questions, you may end up paying far more than you might otherwise.

What Is the Annual Percentage Rate (APR)?

The annual percentage rate (APR) is a major factor to consider when applying for a loan. It represents the interest *plus* all the other costs, such as lender fees and payments for services (escrow, servicing, etc.). The APR on your mortgage is a reflection of what you'll be paying annually for your loan, and it is an especially good way to compare loan officers from different institutions. Remember, the lender is *required by law* to quote the APR when quoting the interest rate.

Is the cost of points included in the APR?
Where the expense of points is divvied up between the
buyer and the seller, your cost will include only the value
of the points paid by you.

Is the lender currently making new mortgage loans?
If not, ask for recommendations of local lenders who are
actively issuing new mortgages. Also, loan officers at savings and loans, commercial banks, mortgage bankers,
credit unions, and other lenders as well as local real estate
brokers can give you information on new financing.

*What is the lender's current rate for "conventional"
financing?*
Conventional financing is the benchmark against which
all other mortgage concepts are measured. The term arose
in the 1930s when the Federal Housing Administration
created the long-term, *self-amortizing* mortgage loan,
which is a loan for 80 percent of the purchase price of the
property.

Is the lender prepared to commit to the rate quoted?
From the day your application is accepted to the day of
closing takes time, and interest rates vary from day to
day. Thus, your rate could *change* at any point along the
way of processing to closing. A reputable lender should be
willing to commit to the rate he quotes and guarantee it
will not go up for a reasonable length of time while the loan
is being seen through to closing.

Are the lender's qualifying policies flexible?
Although there are certain basic requirements that are
common to all lending institutions, who want to make
certain that you are able to repay the loan ultimately and

to make monthly payments in full and on time, no two applicants for a mortgage are alike. Your circumstances and prospects will be different from someone else's, and the right lender should be willing to accommodate them. For example, a young doctor in a residency program may not earn enough to qualify on paper for financing, but his future earning potential is a factor which a lender cannot ignore.

How much mortgage, given an annual income of X dollars, does the lender consider affordable?

Make clear that you are looking for a general figure only, that you understand you can be qualified only after submitting an application.

Is the institution financially stable?

This may be the most important consideration of all. An unstable lender may quickly approve a loan—but it might lack the money to fund it! Another possibility to be aware of is that you might have a loan approved at a certain rate and then find that the lender hasn't the funds available immediately. By the time they do become available, the rate could have escalated.

Does the institution have a good reputation in the area it serves?

Checking up on the institution's reputation is one good way to determine its reliability. Ask friends and relatives, neighbors, coworkers, colleagues, professionals—such as doctors and lawyers—with whom you deal. Be absolutely sure to ask your real estate professional. Remember, you are the *customer*. As a customer, you deserve the best in quality and service.

Will you have the same loan representative from application to closing?

You and your real estate representative should have the option of being able to call your loan representative at any time along the way of processing for a progress update. You want to be sure that your application is being processed locally—not by some loan committee in another town or state.

How soon after approval will your loan be funded?

You want to know that the institution has the money at hand and is going to be ready to release it to you promptly.

What ratio of income to debt does the lender use for fixed-rate and ARMs financing?

Ratio refers to the percentage of your income allocated to pay *all* your various debts, including the monthly payment of the mortgage. Ask also for ratios for different percentages of down payments—5%, 10%, 20%, 30%, 40%, 50%. Different lenders will have different guidelines and different policies, depending on the loan product they are offering. Ratios for fixed-rate mortgages and ARMs are likely to vary as well.

What range of formats and financing does the lender offer?

Ask about FHA and VA financing, graduated payments, ARMs, and other formats.

If interest rates drop between your application and your closing, will your interest rate drop also?

Some lenders will agree not to *raise* the interest rate; that is, they will lock it in for the period between your application and closing, but it is important to ascertain if they

will *also* agree to lower the quoted rate if interest rates
drop.

What, if any, are the prepayment penalties?

Prepayment is the permission to pay down the loan at a
faster rate than originally agreed. Some lenders offer this
feature without charge; others charge a penalty similar to
the early withdrawal penalty on funds in time-deposit
accounts.

Will your loan be assumable?

Today, loans are mostly either not assumable or they are
assumable only by a borrower the lending institution
considers qualified.

Does the lender offer private mortgage insurance?

Private mortgage insurance is a guarantee by a third
party to repay a portion of the loan to the lender if the
borrower defaults. It is usually a requirement for loans
with down payments of less than 20 percent. The borrower pays the fee.

What fee does the lender charge?

Some lenders charge a nonrefundable fee for application.
You want to know if there is an application fee and
whether it is refundable should the application not be
accepted. In addition, a lender will require an appraisal,
for which there will be a fee.

Does the institution have appraisers on its staff?

All institutions require an appraisal of the property. If
the lender has its own appraisers on staff, it is possible
that the property appraisal can be done faster and with
less cost to you. On the other hand, if you must hire your
own independent appraiser, or have the lender pass along

to you a fee for his hiring of an outside appraiser, it costs you in time and money. In addition, a staff appraiser is familiar with the institution's practices, procedures, and standards and can more easily work with them.

The Appraisal

The appraiser's job is to decide the market value of your home. Factors such as the property's physical condition (age, landscaping, improvements, needed repairs, etc.) and its value in relation to other comparable homes recently sold in the immediate vicinity must be examined. To expedite the process, many lending institutions employ their own appraisers as opposed to having to wait for openings on an independent appraiser's schedule.

The major factors used by appraisers to determine the property's value are:

Occupancy Because owner-occupants have a clear interest in maintaining property values, residential mortgages are likely to have a lower rate of interest than investment loans.

Predominant Value Housing patterns follow fairly clear lines. Thus, $50,000 homes are found in $50,000 areas; $100,000 homes are located in $100,000 neighborhoods; $150,000 homes are found in $150,000 sections. It's important for properties to be within the general pricing patterns of their neighborhoods because those that exceed the norm are considered to be overvalued and will be difficult to sell at full market price. An example would be a five-bedroom house with a pool and a tennis court in an area of two- and three-bedroom homes with no pools and conservative features.

Facilities Property values are influenced by the existence or lack of facilities such as sewers, sidewalks, streetlights, and other community improvements.

Improvements Everything but the land itself is considered an improvement—the house or apartment building; outbuildings such as garages or barns; swimming pools and gardens, etc. Each so-called improvement will be evaluated by the appraiser in terms of age and condition. Extra value will be awarded to modernization of any sort, whether in the kitchen, bathroom, additions, or energy efficiency.

FINDING OUT HOW MUCH MORTGAGE YOU MAY QUALIFY FOR

Most lending institutions are willing to give you a free mortgage analysis. Some have special mortgage counselors available either by telephone or by appointment. In order to request a mortgage analysis by a prospective lender, you will need to provide certain information.

Information Needed to Request Free Mortgage Analysis

1. **Income**
   1a. Annual verifiable income . . . . . . $ _____
   1b. Recurring income (interest, dividends, bonuses, commissions, rentals, etc. Alimony and child support are optional) . . . . $ _____

---

2. Expenses

    2a Total credit and charge card
         balances $ _____

    2b Total monthly payments (auto,
         loans) $ _____

    2c Expenses for any property you
         will retain in addition to the pro-
         perty being mortgaged (condo or
         co-op maintenance fees, taxes,
         insurance) . . . . $ _____

3. Down Payment

    Amount of down payment available
    (this can come from cash on hand, equity
    in present home, other properties,
    investments, savings, gifts) . . . . $ _____

4. Market Value of Property . . . . $ _____

THE COMPUTERIZED MORTGAGE

The quest for real estate financing is a complex one. Both the loan search and the loan approval process can now be assisted by computer programs that provide an electronic shopping center for available mortgages. With such a data base, which greatly reduces the number of calls a prospective borrower needs to make, information about various loan formats currently available is gathered at one source. A computer system can display literally hundreds of loans, and looking at so many gives the borrower a good sense of the prevailing market trends and helps pinpoint good deals. In addition to simplifying the search process, the electronic information is *current*, as lenders with new offers or changing rates can update their material constantly.

Mortgage information systems are already in place in many areas with brokers using them to track loans, estimate closing costs, and project how much individual borrowers might be able to afford based on their incomes and debts.

Also, about thirty major institutions have turned to computer programming to make processing of loans fairer and faster by the end of 1992.

WANT MORE INFORMATION?

Money magazine offers a ''Mortgage Match'' kit containing a weekly-updated computer printout of area lenders, with full information on each loan: rates, points, fees, indexes, margins, caps, commitment periods, rate locks, etc. You get a second printout at a time you specify, up to four weeks later, a forty-four-page booklet, ''How to Shop for Your Mortgage,'' and the latest issue of ''Homebuyer News and Tips,'' an informative newsletter. To order your kit, call 1–800–243–8474. Price is $29.95.

APPLYING FOR FINANCING

By the time you are ready to apply for financing, you have probably already signed the sale/purchase contract for the house you plan to buy. A typical contract will have as one of its provisions a specified length of time you have to arrange for your loan and get it approved. This is usually three to six weeks, and it's important to be aware of this deadline. When doing your preliminary scouting of lenders, be sure to ask how long you can expect it to take for approval of your application.

When you go to formally apply for your loan, take your contract with you. In addition, you should bring all of these items listed below to help avoid any delays in processing your application.

As the first document you will be asked to complete is the loan application, which has specific areas for the information required, the entire process may come to a halt if you do not have the proper information and documentation. Therefore, be sure to have *all* of the needed information at hand. If you're uncertain about whether you'll need some piece of information, stay on the safe side and bring it along anyway. Snags caused by missing or improper documentation can be time-consuming and frustrating.

1. Your employment history for the past two years, including employers' addresses and phone numbers, recent pay stubs, and W-2 tax forms. You are not required to list other sources of income, such as alimony or child support, but if you wish to do so, bring the appropriate documentation. Also, if you are planning to list rental income, investment income or dividends, or other secondary sources of income, you will need proper documentation of these sources.

2. Self-employed persons must bring both personal and business tax returns for the preceding two years, or financial statements including profit and loss for a business, income from 1099 copies, and balance sheets for the past two years.

3. The loan agent will want to see all information on your cash assets, including your checking, savings, and retirement accounts. Bring statements, pass-books, or other proof of these assets. Also provide the name and address of each institution where you have cash deposited, along with the account number of each account and its approximate balance.

4. A list of all your personal assets (cars, boats, insurance policies, cash, investments, personal property, etc.), with each item's or group's approximate value.

5. A list of all your creditors, with names, addresses, and account numbers, your total balance owed each, and the approximate monthly payment.

6. If the house you plan to buy is still under construction, you or your builder may be required to submit copies of the plans and specifications.

In addition to the above requirements, which apply to nearly everybody, there are special-case requirements. Below is a comprehensive checklist.

Application Checklist

If Employed
W-2 forms (two years); pay stubs (last thirty days)
Verification of year-to-date income

If Self-employed
Business credit report
Income tax returns (two years)
Form 1099 for commissions
Year-to-date profit and loss statement
Current balance sheet

If Partnership
  Form K-1 (two years)
  Partnership return
  Personal tax return (two years)
If Corporation
  Personal return (two years)
  Form 1120 (two years)
Deposits
  Receipt for deposit on property
  Bank statements
  Stock and bond accounts
Mortgages
  Current mortgage balance
  Mortgage payment record
If Current Home Is to Be Sold
  Evidence of sale or copy of current listing
If Rental Property Is Owned
  Lease and tax information
If Divorced
  Final settlement and alimony payments (if applicable)
If a Gift Is Provided
  Irrevocable gift letter
  Evidence of donor's ability to make gift
  Show relationship to donor, if any
  Donor's name and address

APPROVAL GUIDELINES

In reviewing your application, the lending institution determines how much you can reasonably afford. The monthly housing expenses for your primary residence, including housing expenses for your primary residence, including principal, interest, taxes, insurance, and common charges or maintenance, cannot exceed *28 percent* of your monthly gross income. Monthly payments of your *total* debt (including your new mortgage) cannot exceed *36 percent* of your monthly gross income. Loans exceeding these amounts would have a limit of *33 percent* of your monthly gross income for *total* payments. Of course, every lending institution has its own guidelines, and these may differ considerably.

YOUR FISCAL CHECKUP

The basic application you make is the starting point in the information collection process. Once you have filled in your application and provided all the necessary documentation, the lender will seek to verify each claim made by a prospective borrower.

The lender's loan processing staff should begin immediately to mail out documents requesting verification of the information you have provided. Financial and employment information will be certified. A credit check will be ordered. So will an appraisal of the property.

Once your application is submitted, you will sign forms that authorize the gathering of this data, beginning with the information you have provided. Most of the research time will be spent in substantiating that information.

Your lender will focus on three areas of your financial situation:

1. *Your equity in the property as represented by your down payment*. Your ability to pay the down payment and all closing costs will be supported by the amounts of current checking and savings balances. If the funds are coming from some other source, such as gifts, proceeds from a previous home's sale, the sale of other assets, etc., those sources may have to be verified.

   If part of the down payment is borrowed, lenders will want to know how much, from whom, and under what conditions. It is important to be aware that some loan programs require purchasers to contribute from 5 to 10 percent of the downpayment from *their own funds*. If you are borrowing for the down payment, that naturally increases your debt and will be taken into account accordingly. Also, in some programs, borrowing more than a set limit will disqualify you for the loan entirely.

2. *Your ability to repay your loan.* This will be determined by an evaluation of both your current debts and your current and past income. Verification forms will be sent to your employer, so it is important to be as accurate as possible when stating income amounts and employment dates. Other forms of income you declare may also have to be verified through appropriate inquiries. Individuals who expect a raise, receive bonuses, or work overtime on a consistent basis should report such information.

3. *Your creditworthiness as an indication of your attitude toward financial responsibility*. Creditworthiness will be evaluated on the basis of past

credit history and the types of credit arrangements you currently have. Your lender will want
to know if your accounts are current and if there
are any unexplained repayment lapses or legal
items, tax liens, judgments, etc. A full explanation will be required if you have gone bankrupt or
been foreclosed in the past seven years. If you are
currently a party to a lawsuit or have a judgment
against you, details must be provided. You may
have to explain them in writing.

YOUR CONSUMER SAFEGUARDS

There are required safeguards that respect and protect
your privacy in the gathering and evaluation of your
credit information. Your loan representative will provide
you with advance information and a full explanation of
these when asking for your authorizations.

The Real Estate Settlement Procedures ACT (RE-
SPA) requires the lender to provide you with information
on all known and estimated closing costs. These are standard costs that must be paid at the time of closing. Examples
can include loan origination fees or points, title insurance
fees, settlement or escrow costs, recording fees, and, if applicable, attorney's fees.

Want More Information?

You can write to the U.S. Department of Housing and Urban Development (HUD), Washington, D.C., for a copy of its booklet "Settlement Costs and YOU," which gives an item-by-item explanation of closing costs.

Your *Truth-in-Lending Disclosure* specifies your loan's annual percentage rate, or APR. The APR reflects the total yearly cost of your loan and includes your interest rate as well as other costs associated with obtaining the loan. Because of the inclusion of such costs, your APR figure will be higher than the loan rate you have been quoted.

The following federal agencies are responsible for enforcing the federal Truth in Lending Act, the law that governs credit term disclosure. Any questions concerning compliance with the act by a particular financial institution should be directed to its enforcement agency.

State Member Banks of the Federal Reserve System
Division of Consumer and Community Affairs
Board of Governors of the Federal Reserve System
20th Street and Constitution Avenue, N.W.
Washington, D.C. 20551
(202) 452-3000

National Banks
Consumer Activities Division
Office of the Comptroller of the Currency

490 L'Enfant Plaza, S.W.
Washington, D.C. 20219
(202) 447-1600

Federal Credit Unions
National Credit Union Administration
1776 G Street, N.W.
Washington, D.C. 20456
(202) 357-1065

Federally Insured Non-Member State-Chartered Banks and Savings Banks
Office of Consumer Programs
Federal Deposit Insurance Corporation
550 17th Street, N.W.
Washington, D.C. 20429
(800) 424-5488 or (202) 898-3536

Federally Insured Savings and Loan Institutions and Federally Chartered Savings Banks
Office of Community Investment
Federal Home Loan Bank Board
1700 G Street, N.W.
Washington, D.C. 20552
(202) 377-6237

Mortgage Companies
Division of Credit Practices
Bureau of Consumer Protection
Federal Trade Commission
601 Pennsylvania Avenue, N.W.
Washington, D.C. 20580
(202) 326-3224

Reduced Documentation Mortgages

Some lending institutions offer an alternative to the usual full documentation requirements. These reduced- (or low-) documentation mortgages are designed to reduce the paperwork and speed the process of approval. Whereas a salaried worker who has been on the job for a number of years and is making the down payment from savings would breeze through the application process, the self-employed person might become enmeshed in a maze of paperwork. Reduced documentation loans can help anyone whose financial situation is more complex than average. Reduced documentation mortgages may be for adjustable- as well as fixed-rate and are usually available at the same rate of interest and number of points as full-documentation options. The principal difference between full documentation and low documentation is the amount of the down payment, which is from 20 percent to 30 percent, depending on the amount of the loan. When turning in your signed application, you must provide a contract of sale and the application fee (if applicable), furnish proof of your payment history, and prove that you have the cash for the down payment and closing costs.

FOUR

CLOSING THE DEAL

THE APPROVAL PROCESS

After you have completed all the forms and provided all the necessary information, the application is formally submitted, and the next days will be spent waiting for the replies to come in. During this period, your loan representative may call to request additional information. Remember that mortgages are complex transactions, and there is always the possibility that you may encounter paperwork in addition to the basics given previously. Should your loan officer ask for any further verifications, be sure to respond promptly and accurately. Giving these requests your priority attention could save you many extra days of waiting.

Most service-oriented lending institutions will make

every effort to see that your waiting period is as short as possible. The advantage of having chosen a lender who uses local loan approval (underwriting) is that you aren't going to be waiting for some remotely-located loan committee to get around to vetting your application.

Another point to remember: be sure to ask your lender to provide you with a loan representative who will remain with you through the entire process from application to funding. That way, you and your broker know exactly who to call when questions arise or you want to check on the loan's progress.

The Underwriter

By the time your file reaches the desk of an underwriter—who recommends the decision—it will contain a substantial amount of documentation.

The underwriter's decision will be based entirely upon that documentation.

For this reason, you will want to have provided the fullest and most correct information possible.

When Your Application Is Approved

At this point, the lender will notify you in writing, although you'll probably hear the good news first from your loan representative. Notification may be in the form of a commitment letter which specifies all terms and conditions of the loan. If the lender has guaranteed the rate for a period of time, the letter will include the expiration date of that guarantee. In the absence of such a guarantee, the letter may base terms on the market rate at the date of closing.

The letter could also indicate approval based upon certain conditions (more information may be needed or property improvements may be required). It is imperative that you understand those conditions and immediately take the necessary steps to resolve them.

The same can be said for the entire letter. Make sure you understand everything. If you have questions, talk to your loan representative or your real estate professional. *Closing cannot take place until you have indicated your agreement with the letter in its final form.*

What About Rejection?

If your loan application is denied, the lender must provide you with a reason for the rejection. You may receive a counteroffer to consider or denial may be outright, the result of negative information. You are entitled to know what the information is and who submitted it. If it is inaccurate or misleading, you can take the steps to correct it—and resubmit your application.

CLOSING (OR SETTLEMENT)

"Going to closing" as the final settlement of a real estate deal is the day you take formal possession of your property. Professionals suggest that a buyer visit the property a day or two ahead of closing to make sure everything is in proper order prior to formally taking possession of the new home.

Settlement and *closing* are two names for the same event. Closing, important as it is—the final step in the purchase of your property—is basically an accounting of who owes what to whom as a result of the real estate sale.

Now, the buyer must pay the seller for the property, the seller may have to pay off his own loan, brokerage fees, etc.

In some states, you will be the key attendee of this meeting, joined by your real estate professional and the settlement agent as well as any attorneys involved. Sometimes the seller will also be a participant, particularly if he is assuming any of the closing costs.

Prior to the meeting, the settlement agent will have prepared an estimated *uniform settlement statement*, which lists specifics of your purchase arrangement and all the closing costs now due.

At this time, the transfer taxes, points, adjustments between buyer and seller (as such items as oil in the furnace, prepaid taxes), title insurance, and all other costs are disbursed, being first collected from the parties and then credited as required.

In other states (California, for example), all transactional activity occurs on *the day before* closing, which is the actual day the buyer assumes ownership.

As these activities are expedited by an escrow company acting on behalf of both the buyer and seller, there is no big meeting on closing day; instead, the day itself denotes that all requirements have been fulfilled, all documents have been signed, and all funds have been transferred.

Having discharged its responsibilities, the escrow company officially closes the transaction on closing day.

You, the buyer, are entitled to a full explanation of, and an estimate of, each and every closing cost you will be incurring. Make sure all your questions are answered to your complete satisfaction. You can obtain a copy of HUD's "Settlement Costs and YOU" either from your lender or direct from the Department of Housing and Urban Development, which gives a complete item-by-item explanation of closing costs (see page 57).

Below is a summary of what you can expect to happen

either on closing day or the day prior, depending on where you live.

- The settlement agent will take you point by point through the specifics of the lender's note and the uniform settlement statement.
- Any costs you may owe will be collected. Funds will be disbursed upon the completion of all closing transactions.
- The settlement agent will have verified that all exceptions noted in the commitment letter are cleared so that a title policy ensuring clear title to the property can be issued.
- The settlement agent will follow through with arrangements to record the deed and mortgage in the appropriate public records.

CLOSING COSTS

Although the rate of interest is the primary factor in the minds of most borrowers and it is the way lenders have traditionally made their profits, lenders now derive a growing proportion of their revenues from the fees and charges generated in the granting of new mortgages.

Often, borrowers select one lender over another on the basis of interest rate alone, but additional expenses should also be considered. Today these "extras" can greatly influence the cost of financing, and they are an important factor in judging which loan to choose.

In addition to the possibility of an application fee there are other costs to consider, most of which arise at closing.

- Your credit report is a time-consuming job, and most lenders will charge you a fee for this.

- An appraisal, which is required by all lenders and is a federally mandated licensing requirement for them, is paid for by the borrower. Depending on whether the lender has its own appraiser or hires an outside one, costs will vary. A rule of thumb is that there is often a wait of four to six weeks for an independent appraiser. Buyers usually pay $250–$300 if they are willing to wait. Quicker evaluations are more costly—the shorter the time, the higher the cost.

- Lenders hold in reserve money to pay property taxes, condo fees, or mortgage insurance premiums. This can represent a considerable amount of money at closing, so it is important to compare lender policies regarding this expense.

Points are perhaps the most confusing cost at closing. Another name for a point is *loan discount fee*. A point is equal to 1 percent of a mortgage and is paid or credited to the lender at settlement.

Points are for the purpose of increasing the lender's profit. For example, say you get a $100,000 loan at 10 percent interest. The lender charges you one point, or $1,000.

At settlement, you receive only $99,000. In effect, the lender has loaned you only $99,000, but you must pay the full $100,000 plus interest.

Points are what the lender charges for processing the loan, and they vary in relation to the interest rate. Generally speaking, a lower interest rate will mean more points, while fewer points will indicate a higher interest rate. It's important to calculate the various possible combinations. Another factor to consider is how long you plan to hold the property. Typically, if you plan to own the property only a short time (fifty-four months or less), you are better off with the higher interest rate and fewer points.

There are some rules governing points. With VA loans, the seller must pay all points. With conventional loans, the payment of points is a matter of negotiation. Sellers will sometimes agree to pay a portion of the cost of points.

Points are a complex issue, and it's possible the rules may change in the future. Today, some lending institutions are offering a "no closing costs option." With this option, you do not have to pay points, and some other fees, such as the mortgage recording tax, bank attorney's fee, survey, recording fee, and mortgage title insurance are eliminated.

Different lenders have different policies, and they may vary widely in different parts of the country. Always ask your prospective lender about points and whether you can pay fewer points in exchange for a higher interest rate, or vice versa. And don't forget to consider the length of time you will own the property. Find out how long you must own it in order to justify a higher interest rate with fewer points.

ESTIMATING CLOSING COSTS

In order to be sure you have planned for closing costs and that you will have sufficient funds over and above your down payment to pay them on closing day, refer to the following list of particulars. Note that not all of them are applicable in all states. Ask your real estate professional or your lender to tell you which apply in your area.

1. Deposit $ _____

2. Remainder of Down Payment $ _____

3. Loan Fee (Points) $ _____

4. Prepaid Mortgage Interest $ _____

5. Attorneys' Fees $ _____

6. Recording Fees $ _____

7. Title Search $ _____

8. Title Insurance $ _____

9. Lien Certificate $ _____

10. Escrow/Impound Deposit $ _____

11. Processing Fees $ _____

12. Settlement Agent Fees $ _____

13. Credit Report $ _____

14. Appraisal $ _____

15. Tax Service Fees $ _____

16. Survey $ _____

17. Prepaid Taxes $ _____

18. Private Mortgage Insurance $ _____

19. Underwriting Fees $ _____

20. Warehousing Fees $ _____

21. Other $ _____
    Total $ _____

Another cost to be aware of, though it is not technically a part of closing costs, is the necessity to provide a professional inspector's report showing that the property is free and clear of termites and wood-boring insects. These inspections are ordinarily ordered and paid for by the purchaser and are to be presented at closing.

FIVE

REPAYING
THE MORTGAGE

MONTHLY PAYMENTS

As the choice you make between a fixed-rate and an ARM mortgage will affect your monthly payments over the life of your loan, the decision should be made with careful consideration of your estimated income and expenditures in the foreseeable future, as well as your expectation of length of ownership.

Term of the Loan

Most home mortgage loans are self-amortizing. A loan is considered to be self-amortizing when the monthly payments over the life of the loan are scheduled in such a way to ensure that the loan will be fully repaid by the end of its term. Most home loans are written for fifteen to thirty years, and most are self-amortizing.

If lower monthly payments are important to your budget, and qualifying to carry the amount of the monthly payment is a primary concern, it is advisable to take the longest term available, since a longer term results in lower monthly payments.

On the other hand, if your primary interest is in building equity as quickly as possible while paying the least amount of interest, a fifteen-year term might be your best bet. Although the monthly payment on a shorter-term loan is likely to be somewhat higher than the longer term, the end result is that you will accumulate equity faster and pay less interest. In addition, the interest rate charged on fifteen-year mortgages is usually lower than that on longer terms.

Graduated Payments

The mortgage with graduated payments is especially recommended for families who desire to keep their initial monthly payments as low as possible while still buying a house more in keeping with their long-term plans. A graduated payment mortgage beginning with monthly payments too low to pay out the principal of the loan in its term is advisable for those whose expectations are that family income will rise in coming years. Later, the payments rise according to a preset schedule of increases over a period of two to eight years, increasing to a regular monthly payment that will amortize the principal during the mortgage's term.

PREPAYING THE MORTGAGE AND PENALTY POSSIBILITIES

ARMs may commonly be repaid in whole or in part without penalty. Because the ARM loan is pegged to current interest costs, the lender does not stand to lose if the loan is repaid early, but fixed-rate loans may involve penalties for prepayment. *Always* ask your lender about prepayment fees.

FHA residential loans may be prepaid, in whole or in part, without penalty, at any time during the life of the loan. For complete information on prepayment planning for FHA loans, consult with your lender.

SELLING THE PROPERTY

ARMs, FHA, and VA financing can be assumed by qualified borrowers in most cases. Older conventional loans are frequently assumable at original rates and terms.

The risk is in purchasing a new place before selling the old one. It almost always makes sense not even to shop for a new house until you have a firm contract of sale on your current one. The advantage is that, once you do sell, you can find a new home and close on it quickly. Many lenders will preapprove you for a mortgage of a stipulated amount.

Make sure your agent has ascertained that a prospective buyer will qualify for financing before showing your property.

When selling, be certain that you check with your lender for a complete release of liability and assumption information. There may be charges involved, so ask about them.

SIX

ABOUT REFINANCING

Equity is the key word for homeowners considering refinancing.

To arrive at your equity, you subtract the amount you owe on your mortgage from the current value of your home. Your equity is the value of your home, as if it were a savings account.

Equity in a home accumulates in two ways: 1. The portion of each monthly payment dedicated to paying off your mortgage principal adds to your equity, and 2. if your property appreciates, the added value is also considered equity.

Refinancing is the simple way to access the equity you have in your home. The money you receive through refinancing can be used in any number of ways—for investments, to finance your children's college tuitions, to renovate or build an addition to the current property, or to buy a second home.

However, it is important to remember that *refinancing* does not constitute a *second mortgage*. It is, in effect a *totally new first mortgage*. (A second mortgage is when a single property is used to secure more than one loan. In such a case, should a claim arise, the holder of the first (original) mortgage is paid first, before any claim by a second loan holder is honored. The same applies to any third mortgage, and so on.)

In addition to the use of equity money for such costs as college tuition or remodeling, a common motivation is the opportunity to get a more advantageous mortgage. A better mortgage is generally defined in one of three ways:

- Exchanging a higher interest fixed-rate mortgage for one with a lower rate, which would have the effect of lowering the monthly payment.
- Exchanging an ARM for a fixed-rate mortgage when interest rates are low, which would have the effect of locking in the lower interest rate for the life of the loan.
- Exchanging a long-term thirty-year mortgage for a fifteen-year mortgage, which would have the effect of accruing equity more quickly and, over the life of the loan, cost much less in interest.

All of the above are good and sufficient reasons to refinance—*if* the costs of refinancing, which are similar to the costs of the original mortgage, can be recovered over a satisfactory period of time.

Refinancing costs usually run between 2 and 6 percent of the amount of your new mortgage.

A primary consideration, in addition to the up-front

costs of refinancing, is the probable length of time the borrower plans to stay in the home. It may take a number of years for the new interest rate to become profitable— the entire life of the loan is an important consideration. For example, it may take several years for an interest rate that is two full percentage points lower than the original to pay back the costs of refinancing.

Below is a worksheet that will enable you to evaluate your individual financing situation. Calculating these figures accurately will give you a good basis for your decision about refinancing.

How to Decide Whether You Should Refinance

Part A: List all your possible costs in the spaces below. Consult with your lender to find out if he will allow you to include some or all of these costs in your new mortgage. Note that some of these costs may not be applicable to you or different expenses may be incurred.

Application fee . . . . $_____

Organization fee (Points) . . . . $_____

Title search, title insurance,
    property insurance (if needed) . . . . . $_____

Legal fees (bank/personal attorneys). . . $_____

Mortgage tax (if applicable) . . . . $_____

Mortgage recording tax, survey,
    credit reports . . . . $_____

      TOTAL REFINANCING COST   _____

Part B: How to calculate your monthly savings:

STEP 1: Current monthly mortgage payment, minus property taxes, insurance, maintenance is $ _____

STEP 2: New monthly mortgage payment will be: (Use the chart below to figure this.) $_____

       TOTAL MONTHLY SAVINGS $_____

Part C: Divide **A** into **B** to get the number of months it will take for refinancing to be profitable.

     A _____   **B** _____ = $ _____

ESTIMATING PAYMENTS
ON A FIXED-RATE LOAN

To use this table, find the interest rate and the corresponding payment rate for the term of years you want. Multiply the figure in the term-of-years column by the number of thousands of dollars you plan to borrow; for example, if you have been quoted an interest rate of 11 percent for thirty years on $100,000, you would multiply 9.53 by 100, giving a total approximate monthly payment of $953.00.

Interest Rate %	Payment Rate	
	Fifteen Years	Thirty Years
7	$8.99	$6.66
7.25	9.13	6.83
7.5	9.28	7.00
7.75	9.42	7.17
8	9.56	7.34
8.25	9.71	7.52
8.5	9.85	7.69
8.75	10.00	7.87
9	10.15	8.05
9.25	10.30	8.23
9.5	10.45	8.41
9.75	10.60	8.60
10	10.75	8.78
10.25	10.90	8.97
10.5	11.06	9.15
10.75	11.21	9.34
11	11.37	9.53

How Much Can You Save?

With mortgage rates suddenly lower than they have been in over a decade, chances are that if you took out a mortgage over the last twelve years, you are paying higher monthly payments than you have to. For example, if you took out an original mortgage of $125,000 for 360 months at 10.5 percent APR, your monthly payments would be approximately $1,143.42. By refinancing $125,000 for 360 months at 8.5 percent APR you would reduce your monthly payments to $961.14, a difference of $182.28 per month or $2,187.36 over a year. Thus, your savings over the first ten years would be $21,873.60.

ABOUT HOME EQUITY

How Much Can You Borrow?

What you can borrow will be determined both by your equity and the current value of your home. To judge how much your home is worth today, call your local Board of Realtors. Ask for recent sales prices of several houses in your neighborhood that are about the same size, age, and condition as yours. Also ask how long it took to sell them, how many houses were listed locally over the past thirty days, and how many sold. If the average number of days houses have remained on sale is declining, chances are the prices are in good shape. However, if more than six houses came into the market for every one sold, prices are probably not going up soon.

WHAT YOU SHOULD KNOW ABOUT HOME EQUITY LINES OF CREDIT

More and more lenders are offering home equity lines of credit. By using the equity in your home, you may qualify for a sizable amount of credit, available for use when and how you choose, at an interest rate that is relatively low.

For persons in the market for credit, a home equity plan may be right for you or not. Before putting your house on the line—for failure to repay could mean loss of your home—consider the credit terms that best meet your needs.

What Is a Home Equity Line of Credit?

A home equity line is a form of revolving credit in which your home serves as collateral. Because the home is likely to be a consumer's largest asset, many homeowners use their home equity credit lines only for major items such as education, home improvements, or medical bills, not for day-to-day expenses.

With a home equity line, you will be approved for a specific amount of credit—your credit limit—meaning the maximum amount you can borrow at any one time while you have the plan.

Many lenders set the credit limit on a home equity line by taking a percentage (usually 75 percent) of the appraised value of the home and subtracting the balance owed on the existing mortgage.

See the table below for an example of how much you can borrow.

EXAMPLE:
How To Determine Your Credit Line

Current Value of Your Home	$200,000
Multiply by 75%	$150,000
Outstanding Balance on First Mortgage	$ 55,000
Potential Credit Line	$ 95,000

COMPARING A LINE OF CREDIT AND A TRADITIONAL SECOND MORTGAGE

If you are thinking about a home equity line of credit, you might also want to consider a more traditional second mortgage loan. This type of loan provides you with a fixed amount of money repayable over a fixed period. Usually, the payment schedule calls for equal payments that will pay off the entire loan within that time. You might consider a traditional second mortgage loan instead of a home equity line if, for example, you need a set amount for a specific purpose, such as an addition to your home.

When deciding which type of loan best suits your needs, consider the costs under the two alternatives. Look at the APR and other charges. You cannot, however, simply compare the APR for a traditional mortgage loan with the APR for a home equity line because the APRs are figured differently.

- The APR for a traditional mortgage takes into account the interest rate charged plus points and other finance charges.
- The APR for a home equity line is based on the periodic interest rate alone. It does not include points or other charges.

SEVEN

MORTGAGES AS INVESTMENTS

SECONDARY LENDERS

Primary lenders are familiar to anyone who has ever applied for a mortgage—local financial institutions such as savings and loans and commercial banks issue mortgages and collect the payments. The secondary lenders—multibillion-dollar organizations—are less well-known.

Primary lenders sell their mortgages, in order to raise new funds, to *secondary lenders* including the Federal National Mortgage Association (Fannie Mae), the Government National Mortgage Association (Ginnie Mae), and the Federal Home Loan Mortgage Corporation (Freddie Mac).

Fannie Mae

Although Fannie Mae was originally a governmental agency, it was transferred to the private sector. Now a publicly held company, Fannie Mae purchases conventional, FHA, and VA mortgages, ARMS, and second mortgages. It maintains a loan portfolio that includes over a billion dollars in mortgages. Also, Fannie Mae has approximately $430 billion in mortgage-backed securities that are available directly to private investors through their brokers.

Ginnie Mae

Ginnie Mae is part of the Department of Housing and Urban Development (HUD). It assembles and guarantees pools of FHA and VA mortgages. Ginnie Mae issues pass-through certificates, on which investors receive monthly payments for both interest and principal. Approximately $400 billion of these are currently outstanding. For information about Ginnie Mae, you can write to Mr. Laverne Johnson, 451 7th St., S.W., Room 6210, Washington, D.C. 20410-9000. The agency offers several publications and information pamphlets without charge.

Freddie Mac

Freddie Mac is the leading issuer of conventional mortgage-backed securities in the United States. In 1970, Congress chartered Freddie Mac in order to increase the availability of funds for mortgage loans to home buyers. Freddie Mac purchases residential mortgages from lenders and creates mortgage-related securities for investors in the secondary mortgage market. A selected group of dealers, to whom Freddie Mac auctions off its products, sells Mortgage Participation Certificates (PCs), Real Estate Mortgage Investment Conduits (REMICs), and other securities to the public. The common stock trades publicly and is listed on the New York and Pacific Stock Exchanges under the symbol "FRE."

In 1971, Freddie Mac introduced the first conventional mortgage-backed security, called the PC. After residential mortgages are purchased from lenders, Freddie Mac pools mortgages with similar characteristics and sells pieces of this pool in the form of securities to investors. Monthly principal and interest payments on the underlying mortgages are passed through to PC holders. Freddie Mac has $385 billion in outstanding PCs, of which $105 billion are committed to REMICs. Freddie Mac purchases mortgages for cash from many lenders. It pools these mortgages, which include fifteen- and thirty-year fixed-rate and ARMs.

In 1990, the distribution of fixed-versus adjustable-rate mortgages was 77.8 percent fixed and 22.2 percent ARMs. The ARMs percentage has been steadily declining since, with 1991's figure at only 7.4 percent and the first half of 1992 at .04 percent.

A 1991 report from the U.S. Treasury gave Freddie Mac an "A+" rating, assigned by Standard and Poor's as if Freddie Mac had no government sponsorship.

All of Freddie Mac's products and programs are discussed in detail in the related offering circulars, supplements, and fact sheets which are available through Freddie Mac's Investor Inquiry service at 1-800-336-3672, or write to them at 8200 Jones Branch Drive, McLean, VA 22102.

WHO SHOULD INVEST IN MORTGAGES?

Investing in mortgages is like making any other investment, and the same precautions and procedures should
be followed. However, investing in mortgages provides
the investor with protection, as the financial qualification
standards assure that loans will be made only to financially able purchasers. In addition, the national market-
place created by the secondary lenders creates an element
of liquidity—mortgages can quickly be converted to cash
at a reasonable value. Lastly, the national mortgage mar-
ketplace allows local lenders to perceive their mortgage
portfolio as a potential profit source because loans can be
regarded as commodities that can be bought or sold or
retained for profit.

EIGHT

A WORD ABOUT TAXES

PRIMARY RESIDENCE

Historically, deductibility of mortgage interest on the average American home has been considered part of the national heritage. Tax deductions are crucial to homeowners because in effect they reduce the cost of interest. For example, if you are in a 28 percent tax bracket and you have a loan at 10 percent interest, your true financing cost is only 7.2 percent.

Today, if you acquired your mortgage on or before October 13, 1987, the mortgage interest is 100 percent deductible on your 1040 form.

However, if you signed for your mortgage after the above date, some restrictions are applicable.

Interest on principal above $1 million is not deductible.

Points

Points (which are a payment for the use of money) used for the purchase of a new home are currently fully deductible *in the year in which they are paid*. However, there is some possibility that the rules may be changed. Therefore, it's usually a good idea to schedule an appointment with a tax attorney or adviser when considering a mortgage.

RENTAL PROPERTY

Mortgage interest on a home you rent is deductible. You claim this deduction on Schedule E of form 1040.

VACATION HOMES

The tax treatment on a vacation home varies depending on how you use it. There are three categories: 1. you use it personally 100 percent of the time; 2. you rent it out; or 3. some combination of the first two.

> 1. Mortgage interest and property taxes paid on a second home are fully deductible, but points are deducted over the life of the loan. You can rent the property for as long as fourteen days a year as well—and the rest you receive is completely tax

free. Mortgage interest and property taxes are deductible (but not repairs).

2. Rental property, which provides you with income, is treated differently. Expenses such as repairs are deductible as is depreciation, but not mortgage interest.

3. If you rent fifteen days or more, your rental income is taxable, but you can deduct expenses such as utilities, repairs, insurance, and depreciation in proportion to the length of time you rent the house. For example, if you use it yourself for thirty days and rent it for sixty days, you can deduct two-thirds of the expenses. However, if you use the place for more than fourteen days a year, or for more than 10 percent of the number of days it's rented, your deductions cannot exceed the rental income and generate a tax loss.

As with all tax matters, it is a wise idea to check with your personal tax adviser for precise information about your own particular situation.

REFINANCING

The current tax laws on the refinancing of a primary residence allow interest deductibility only up to $100,000 over the amount of the original mortgage, unless the money is used to buy a tax-exempt investment. All other uses of the money allow you to deduct the interest. If you borrow money to make a taxed investment, the interest is still deductible.

About points: The Internal Revenue Service has consistently ruled that points on refinancing are not deductible but must be amortized over the life of the loan. However, confusion frequently arises over whether amounts paid by consumers are actually points or other fees. To cope with this situation and minimize disputes over the deductibility of points paid in connection with the acquisition of a principal residence (not refinancing), the IRS has issued revenue procedures to clarify the questions. Write for IRS Revenue Procedure 92-11, 92-12, and Revenue Rule 92-2.

RESIDENTIAL VERSUS INVESTMENT PROPERTY

Owners of residential property used for no purpose other than personal housing are not allowed to claim deductions for depreciation, maintenance, utilities, repairs, etc. Investors, however, are allowed to claim such deductions.

While residential owners may move from one personal property to another of equal or greater value and defer all taxes from the sale of the first house, investors must pay taxes whenever they sell at a profit.

Personal property owners who are over the age of fifty-five when they sell their homes may claim a one-time profit exclusion of up to $125,000 when they sell. Investors have no such exclusion factor.

How to Get More Information

Write to the IRS (Internal Revenue Service) in Washington, D.C., and ask for a copy of IRS Publication #545, entitled "Interest Expense."

Glossary

Amortization (see also Negative Amortization) The calculation used to determine the amount of equal principal and interest payments needed to pay off a loan within a certain specified period of time. Most first mortgages are amortized over fifteen or thirty years.

Annual Percentage Rate (APR) The total amount of the finance charge, including interest, points, and all loan fees (i.e., escrow, processing, etc.), calculated as a percentage of the borrowed amount and expressed as a yearly rate.

Application Fee A fee that may be charged by the lender to cover the costs of processing your loan application. It is usually charged at the beginning of the application process.

Appraisal 1. The professional examination of property for the purpose of estimating its current market value. 2. The written report of same.

Appraisal Fee The fee you pay to have a property appraised.

Assessed Value The value placed on property by the tax assessor to determine property taxes.

Assumability (Assumption of a mortgage or Assumption of a deed of trust) Agreement by a buyer to assume liability under an existing agreement between seller and lender.

Not all loans or loan terms are "assumable." The lender typically must approve the new borrower.

Assumption Fee The fee you pay the lender in order to assume someone else's mortgage loan.

Balloon Payment When monthly payments are not sufficient to amortize the loan, there is a large, or *balloon*, payment to be made in a lump sum when the loan term ends. Sometimes the balloon payment is written into the mortgage loan; such should be avoided.

Binder Written evidence of insurance, which covers a limited time: to be replaced later with a permanent policy.

Blanket Mortgage A single mortgage secured by several properties.

Broker See Mortgage Broker and Real Estate Broker.

Caps See Rate Cap and Payment Cap.

Closing The final procedure in a real estate transaction; when documents are executed and/or recorded, title is transferred from seller to buyer, funds are disbursed, and the sale is completed.

Closing Costs Buyer's and seller's expenses incidental to the sale and purchase of real estate, such as title fees, loan fees, etc.

Closing Statement A statement prepared by attorney, broker, escrow company, or lender, giving a complete itemization of costs incurred in a real estate transaction. A separate statement is prepared for the buyer and seller.

Condominium A structure of two or more units, the interior space (including the wall coverings but not the walls) of each unit being individually owned; the balance of the structure and the land is owned in common by all the unit owners.

Conveyance 1. Transfer of title. 2. The document, such as a deed, by which the title is officially transferred.

Co-op (Co-operative housing) A structure of two or more units that is owned by a corporation made up (typically) of the occupants. As such, no real property is owned by the individuals, only shares in the corporation allocated to particular apartments.

Credit Limit The maximum amount that you can borrow under the home equity plan.

Curtailment A payment that either shortens or pays off a mortgage in full. If you pay off your entire balance in one payment, the loan has been curtailed.

Deed of Trust (or Trust deed) Used in place of a mortgage in some states. Title is transferred to a trustee by the borrower, with the lender as beneficiary, until the loan balance has been paid.

Deferred Interest See Negative Amortization.

Earnest Money Deposit of money accompanying an offer to buy property, to show good faith.

Effective Age Age of a structure as estimated by its condition rather than actual age. Takes into account rehabilitation and maintenance.

Escrow 1. The temporary holding by a third (neutral) party of deposited funds pending completion of agreed terms in a sales contract. 2. In some states, all instruments necessary to the sale are delivered to a third party with instructions as to their use. 3. The term "in escrow" is used in some areas to refer to the time from completion of sales contract to transfer of title. Escrow fees are usually considered part of closing costs.

Escrow Account See Impound Account.

Escrow Company A company established to perform escrow services.

Equity The difference between the fair market value (the appraised value) of your home and your outstanding mortgage balance.

Factor See Margin.

Hazard Insurance Insurance protection for the borrower and the lender against the property loss due to fire, wind, or natural hazards. Many lenders require payment of the first year's premium as part of the closing costs.

Home Equity Loan A loan secured against your equity in the property. See Refinance.

Home Inspection Service A service performed by a contractor or experienced individual or company; the purpose is to detect and diagnose defects in a property and generally evaluate its condition.

Impound Account (also called Escrow Account in some states) An account held by the lender for payment of taxes, insurance, and other periodic debts against a property. The borrower pays a specific amount over and above the monthly loan payment, and the lender pays the bills with the accumulated funds. Some lenders require an impound account for certain types of financing.

Index A published interest rate composite used by lenders. Its movements determine interest adjustments on adjustable-rate mortgages (ARMs).

Lien A claim against a property in satisfaction of a debt. It can be voluntary, such as a mortgage, or involuntary, as for back taxes.

Listing 1. A property listed for sale. 2. A contract between a seller and a real estate broker.

Loan-to-Value (LTV) Ratio The amount of the loan as a percentage of the property's appraised value. An 80 percent loan, for example, is determined by subtracting a 20 percent down payment from the property's appraised value.

Locking In Mortgage rates can change daily. An advertised rate may not be the rate you finally get. Borrowers must ask lenders when a rate is "locked in," or guaranteed for a specified period of time.

Margin The margin is the difference between the ARM index and the rate the lender charges. Example: an index rate of 8 percent, plus a margin of 2.5 percent, could result in home loan rate of 10.5 percent. In some areas, the margin is referred to as the factor. The fixed margin over the index covers the lender's operating expenses and profit margin.

Market Value The current value of real estate that a buyer is willing to pay and a seller is willing to accept.

Mortgage Evidence of the security for a loan. It is the document, signed by the borrower, which gives the lender the right to the property if the borrower fails to live up to the loan arrangement.

Mortgage Broker Individuals or institutions who match those who need money with interested investors.

Multiple Listing An exclusive listing, submitted to all members of an association, so that each may have an opportunity to sell the property.

Multiple Listing Service (MLS) A real estate service that advises brokers of properties that are for sale.

Negative Amortization (see also Amortization) Occurs when the minimum monthly payment on an adjustable-rate mortgage is not large enough to cover the full amount of interest that is due. The difference between interest owed and interest paid may then be added to the loan's principal balance at the option of the borrower.

Origination Fee(s) (see also Point) Also called a Loan Fee, this is a fee assessed by the lender for processing the loan. Most lenders' charges are based upon the amount of the loan, and one point equals 1 percent of the loan amount. These fees are normally paid by the borrower at closing. In some cases, however, they may be paid by the seller or shared by both parties. Also, the lender may allow the charges to be deducted from the mortgage amount.

Payment Cap Places an annual limit on the amount that a monthly payment can increase. This feature is offered by some ARM lenders instead of an annual interest rate cap.

Point An amount equal to 1 percent of the principal balance of a mortgage loan. (Two points equal 2 percent of the balance, etc.) See Origination Fees.

Prepayment Penalty A fee charged by some lenders when the loan is repaid prior to maturity.

Private Mortgage Insurance (PMI) Mortgage default insurance designed to pay the lender a portion of the outstanding balance of a loan in the event that the homeowner defaults. PMI may be required on certain types of loans. If so, the initial premium is usually one of the closing costs, while subsequent premiums are included in the borrower's monthly payments. Usually applies to loans with 10 percent or less down payment.

Rate Cap The rate cap defines rate limits, either from one adjustment period to the next or over the life of the loan.

Real Estate Agent A person licensed by the state who represents a broker in real estate transactions.

Real Estate Broker Buyers and sellers are commonly dependent on real estate brokers to locate real estate financing and to advise them on current rates, points, and loan formats. They commonly represent the *seller* of a property. Commercial real estate brokers often perform the services of mortgage brokers.

Recording and Transfer Fees Charges for recording documents with public agencies. These may also be included in the borrower's closing costs. A document tax is charged in some states on real estate transactions.

Refinance The securing of a new loan either to pay off an existing lien or mortgage on the property or to access your equity.

Restructure A loan that remains in place but for which new terms have been negotiated. For example, if monthly payments are increased by a specified amount for the term of the loan, it has been restructured.

Self-Amortization Occurs when the monthly payments ensure that the loan is fully paid at the end of its term.

Settlement See Closing.

Settlement Statement See Closing Statement.

Survey May be required by the title company to ensure that the house is properly situated on the property. A survey is intended to reveal if the house, fence, pool, or patio are built on or too near adjoining property or utility easements. Fees, if any, are normally paid by the borrower.

Title Ownership or proof of ownership to real property.

Title Company A company that issues title insurance. In some areas, title companies also perform escrow functions.

Title Insurance Insurance protection against the consequences of a preexisting lien or encumbrance on a property that might be discovered after a change in ownership.

Trust Deed See Deed of Trust.

Underwriting Standards set by the lender that the borrower must meet in order to qualify for the loan.

Variable Rate An interest rate that changes periodically in relation to an index. Payments may increase or decrease.

Vesting Conveying ownership.

Recommended Reading

Miller, Peter G. *The Common-Sense Mortgage*. New York: Harper Perennial, 1992.
———. *Buy Your First Home Now*. New York: Harper Perennial, 1990.
Thomsett, Michael. *The Complete Guide to Selling Your Home*. New York: Dow Jones–Irwin, 1991.